THE
LEPRECHAUN
LIBRARY

EGGS

Linda Sonntag

The Leprechaun Library
published by
G.P.PUTNAM'S SONS
NEW YORK

THE EGG DANCE

Lightly, nimbly, quickly, and with hairsbreadth accuracy, she carried on the dance. She skipped so sharply and surely along between the eggs, and trod so closely down beside them, that you would have thought every instant she must trample one of them in pieces, or kick the rest away in her rapid turns. By no means! She touched no one of them, though winding herself through their mazes with all kinds of steps, wide and narrow, nay even with leaps, and at last half kneeling.

Constant as the movement of a clock, she ran her course; and the strange music, at each repetition of the tune, gave a new impulse to the dance, recommencing and again rushing off as at first . . .

The dance being ended, she rolled the eggs together softly with her foot into a little heap, left none behind, harmed none; then placed herself beside it, taking the bandage from her eyes, and concluding her performance with a little bow.

GOETHE: WILHELM MEISTER

2

RECORD EGGS

The largest egg in the world is laid by the ostrich. It can measure up to 8 in (20 cm) in length and 6 in (15 cm) in diameter and its volume is equal to that of two dozen hens' eggs. It is considered a great delicacy by the Egyptian vulture – but its shell is strong enough to support a 20-stone man, and so the vulture has had to learn how to crack the shell by hitting it with a rock which he drops from his beak. The ostrich egg, should you want to eat one for breakfast, takes 40 minutes to boil.

The Princess Te Kawan is the hen who holds the record for egg-laying. She is a Black Orpington who managed to produce 361 eggs in 364 days. The highest number of yolks found in an egg is nine.

Humans also claim to have broken records with eggs. An egg has been dropped 600 feet (183 m) and remained intact, and another was thrown 350 feet (106 m) without harm. The longest egg-and-spoon race was a 27-mile (44 km) marathon which lasted 4 hours 17 minutes.

Other people have set out to break eggs as well as records. Two blind men shelled 1050 dozen in a 7¼-hour shift in a hotel restaurant. The record for eating eggs is equally astonishing: 14 hard-boiled in 58 seconds, 32 soft-boiled in 78 seconds and an amazing 13 raw in 2.2 seconds. Absolutely eggstraordinary!

> Humpty Dumpty lay in the beck,
> With all his sinews around his neck;
> All the King's surgeons, and all the King's wrights,
> Could not put Humpty Dumpty to rights.

During the Civil War when the Royalists were garrisoned at Oxford, an inventor of war machines called Dr Chillingworth was introduced to King Charles I. These machines were all the rage on the Continent and Charles was persuaded that it would be a good idea to use one against the Roundhead stronghold in Gloucester. The river Severn had to be crossed before the city walls could be reached, and this would obviously entail a substantial loss of life, so Dr Chillingworth invented a wheeled contraption which would roll downhill and, gathering momentum, propel itself across the river. It was built on similar lines to the Roman battle formation known as the 'tortoise', and the troops christened it Humpty Dumpty. By the time it was ready to roll and packed with men-at-arms the Roundheads had got wind of it and widened the river. So Humpty collapsed in mid-stream, drowning large numbers of soldiers.

There are other reasons why Humpty has come to be known as a human egg. A humpty-dumpty was a popular seventeenth-century egg and brandy drink, and also the nickname for a fat person of either sex. There used to be a nursery game in which the players sat with their skirts clasped round their ankles. The idea was to fall backwards and right yourself again without overbalancing.

All these strands, now mostly forgotten, have come together to produce one of our best-loved nursery rhymes:

> Humpty Dumpty sat on a wall,
> Humpty Dumpty had a great fall.
> All the King's horses and all the King's men,
> Couldn't put Humpty together again.

THE GOOSE THAT LAID THE GOLDEN EGGS

There once was a man who was blessed with the possession of a miraculous goose. Each day it delighted him by laying a golden egg, so that soon its owner was very rich indeed. But the man was greedy: the more gold he had, the more he wanted.

Growing impatient with only one egg a day he decided to cut open the goose, as he believed that a whole horde of golden eggs was concealed inside it. So he killed the poor goose, but when he opened her up he found nothing; his magical bird was only like any other goose inside and in his greed and impatience he had lost a valuable friend.

AESOP

EASTER RITUALS

Much of the ritual carried on at Easter-time centres around the egg. One ancient custom which seems to be enjoying a new lease of life is pace-egging. ('Pace' comes from the Latin word 'pascha', meaning 'Easter'.) This is performed mainly by men who dress up in ribbons and rags and strips of coloured paper. One blackens his face, though the effect is often grisly enough as it is, and acts as 'tosspot'. He carries a basket on his arm and intimidates the villagers into tossing eggs into it, though money is always a welcome substitute. The pace-eggers enact a play and then collect their reward. If they meet a rival band of egg-gatherers in the street they challenge each other with wooden swords (and do not always escape unscathed).

An Easter game popular in many countries is egg-tapping, a messier version of conkers which produces champion eggs to be displayed and admired all year. Another form of this which allows children to exercise their sadistic tendencies is where the egg is bashed on the opponent's forehead – and masochists even try to break their eggs on their own skulls.

A slightly more civilized custom is egg-rolling, a sort of bowls. This practice commemorates the rolling away of the stone from the mouth of Christ's tomb, and is played to this day on the lawns of the White House – though to preserve the grass and the competitor's footwear plastic eggs are used in place of the real thing.

EGG SUPERSTITIONS

If a man wants to discover the identity of a witch, he should take an Easter egg into church with him. If there are any witches in the congregation he will recognize them because they will have pieces of pork in their hands instead of prayer books and milk pails on their heads instead of bonnets.

If a girl wants to know whom she will marry, she should boil an egg, fast for a day, then extract the yolk and fill the cavity with salt. She must then eat the whole (including the shell) and walk backwards muttering an incantation to St Agnes. If she takes a drink before sunrise the spell will be broken and her lover's identity will remain unrevealed.

In China, eggs are the pre-eminent symbol of life and re-birth, and so to announce the arrival of new offspring families paint eggs bright red – the colour of happiness. This long-established practice is said to ensure good luck for the new-born child.

So then the mother of the water, mother of the water,
    virgin of the air,
Raised her knee from the sea, her shoulder blade from a
    billow,
For the goldeneye as a place for a nest, as an agreeable
    dwelling place;
That goldeneye, graceful bird, flits about, soars about.
She discovered the knee of the mother of the water on the
    bluish open sea;
She thought it a grass grown tussock, fresh turf.
She soars about, flits about, settles down on the knee.
On it she builds her nest, laid her golden eggs,
Six golden eggs, the seventh an iron egg.
She began to brood the eggs, to warm the top of the knee.
She brooded one day, brooded a second, then brooded a
    third too.
Now because of that the mother of the water, mother of the
    water, virgin of the air,
Feels burning hot, her skin scorched;
She thought her knee was burning, all her sinews melting.
Suddenly she twitched her knee, made her limbs tremble.
The eggs tumbled into the water, are sent into the waves of
    the sea;
The eggs cracked to pieces, broke to bits.
The eggs do not get into the ooze, the bits not get mixed up
    with the water.
The bits were turned into fine things, the pieces into
    beautiful things:
The lower half of one egg into the earth beneath,
The top half of another egg into the heaven above.
The top half of one yolk gets to glow like the sun,
The top half of one white gets to gleam palely as the moon;
Any mottled things on an egg, those become stars in
    heaven,
Anything black on an egg, those indeed become clouds in
    the sky.

KALEVALA

EGGS FOR EASTER

Easter is a Christian festival, but its origin, and the custom of giving Easter eggs, have roots which stretch far back into pagan tradition.

Some say that the English word 'Easter' itself derives from the Saxon 'oster', meaning 'to rise'. It was an old Aryan belief that the sun rose on Easter Day and its appearance was greeted with much dancing and celebration. The new sun was symbolized by red and gold eggs, which were exchanged to commemorate its birth.

More recently eggs have been given in remembrance of Christ's Resurrection. Nuns living near Rome would decorate hens' eggs and take them to the church on Easter Sunday to be blessed by the priests. At dinner that day they would form the centrepiece of a banquet of spring foods.

The giving of Easter eggs often has amorous rather than relgious overtones. In Czechoslovakia and Hungary girls colour and decorate eggs for their sweethearts. If a man receives a large number of eggs on Easter Day he is considered a good catch. He will put the eggs away for some time to test the strength of their donors' love. The egg whose colouring does not fade belongs to the girl he will marry. Girls can hedge their bets by giving eggs to more than one man, but their Alsatian counterparts have no such luck. They have to wait for their menfolk to collect the eggs they have decorated. A girl whom no one favours is left with her eggs and told to hatch them out herself.

DECORATED EGGS

Legend has it that the tradition of decorating eggs started with the birth of Christ. The Virgin is said to have painted eggs red, yellow and green to delight her baby.

Lucky owners of the araucana hen, popular today in the USA as a pet, have a ready supply of coloured Easter eggs because this unique bird lays eggs of either pink, blue or green. But most people still have to colour their own. A white hen's egg is best, and one of the simplest dyes is onion peel, which can produce yellow, red and brown. The peel can be soaked for several days in tepid water before the eggs are boiled in it, or it can be wrapped round the egg to produce a tie-dye effect. Many natural substances from wood shavings to wolf's milk and beetroot to birch leaves can be used to create a whole range of colours in a similar way. A design can then be scratched on the egg with an old-fashioned school pen.

Another way of decorating coloured eggs is with appliqué – anything including pastry, wool, sea shells and paper shapes can be stuck on to egg shells. Reeds are particularly popular in many countries as they are thought to be lucky. A reed, once dried, will turn green again if soaked with rain, and hence is a symbol of immortality. Since the Easter egg symbolizes the Resurrection, the two are particularly suited.

TRICKS WITH EGGS

Eggs have long been popular with magicians, who love to produce them from their sleeves, from behind their ears, or merely out of thin air. A favourite, though not very refined, trick was to coax a whole stream of eggs from an assistant's mouth. At the time, this was said to be unsuited 'for indiscriminate performance, but highly appreciated by juvenile or bucolic spectators'.

Originally this trick was done with a real egg, but the conjuror was warned that his assistant was in danger of choking if surprised by a sudden attack of coughing or laughter, and so a half-shell of celluloid was developed which could be stuck on the end of the tongue and shown to the audience as many times as they liked, while the magician 'palmed' the actual egg in front of their eyes.

One of the most celebrated egg tricks of all time was performed by Christopher Columbus. On returning to the Spanish court after his discovery of the West Indies, he was much fêted by all present, to the discomfiture of one particularly jealous courtier. This man decided to take the explorer down a peg or two by asking whether he thought there were not other Spaniards who could have done as well. Instead of replying immediately, Columbus took out an egg which he had handy in his pocket and invited the company to make it stand on end. Everyone tried, though no one succeeded. Columbus then struck the egg upon the table so that the end broke and the egg was left standing on the broken part. Thus he proved that once he had shown the way to the New World, nothing was easier than to follow it.

EASTER MESSAGES

In Germany it has long been the tradition to exchange eggs at Easter which are inscribed with significant messages rather than just prettily decorated. In the Tyrol this is a popular custom amongst lovers, but the gift does not always signify a betrothal: if a young man receives a pair of eggs he knows his sweetheart has transferred her affections elsewhere and will therefore dash the eggs to the ground in despair.

For Easter you will get this egg
For Whitsun my promise,
For Shrovetide my hand,
That I promise you.

See, you have an egg!
I know you would rather have two.
But I would be a fool;
You and I would still not be as one.

You old ass,
Stay at home.
I give you a pair of Easter eggs.
Love is gone.

Sweet is what this egg conceals,
But sweeter far a kiss from you.

Even if distant places part us,
Remain in love
With the one who wrote these words
Upon this Easter egg.

If this egg were my heart,
I certainly would not give it to you.

THE WITCH'S BOAT

There was once a gypsy girl who was very curious. One day she ate an egg and left the shell on the riverbank to see what would happen. When night fell a witch came and said a magic word. The egg shell turned into a beautiful boat which carried the witch away – down the river and across the ocean to foreign shores. The girl remembered the word and the next time she ate an egg she made herself a boat. She sailed to strange lands and came back laden with exotic flowers and fruit which she sold to her neighbours.

One of these neighbours was a wicked woman and jealous of the girl's success. She hid behind the bushes on the riverbank and watched for her return. When night fell the wicked woman crept into the boat and bade it take her to lands rich in silk and gold. But she didn't know the magic word and the boat started to sink. Then the woman cried out in a great rage: 'In God's name get on with you!' At this the spell was broken, the boat turned back into an egg shell and the woman was drowned in the great rolling sea.

SLAVONIAN GYPSY TALE

THE EASTER HARE

The pagan goddess Eastre or Eostre (Spring or Dawn, according to legend) is often credited with having given her name to the Easter festival. Her favourite animal was the hare, who represents love, fertility and growth.

The hare and the egg have been closely associated since the beginning of time. One Noah's Ark story tells how when the floods came, Noah gathered together all the birds and the beasts and set sail with his family in an egg shell. The shell sprang leaks repeatedly and the ark with its precious cargo of life was in danger of sinking – until Noah plugged the leak with the tail of a hare and all were saved.

In Germany children are taught to believe that the hare lays their Easter eggs, and they make a soup of green leaves to entice her to the special nests they have built for her in the garden. The hare even colours her own eggs, lighting bonfires to obtain dyes from flowers and grasses. If a child is naughty, the hare will leave nothing but droppings in its nest. The luckiest child is the one whose Easter egg hatches – the baby bird inside will be born with the head of a hare.

The legend of the hare laying eggs is not as absurd as it sounds. Plovers make their nests on the ground, often near a hare's form. If the hare has deserted its form, the plover will often convert it: so if eggs can be laid in a hare's nest, why not by the hare itself?

Fröhliche O·S·T·E·R·N

THE TWO RATS, THE FOX AND THE EGG

Two rats were looking for food, and they found an egg. The dinner was sufficient for two animals of their size: two rats, after all, do not need an ox to satisfy their appetites. Ravenous, they attacked the egg, one from each side. Then Master Fox appeared. Oh, what an inconvenient encounter! How could they save the egg? For to carry it away they would have to hold it with their front feet, then either roll it or pull it – and that was an impossible, not to say hazardous, task.

Necessity provided them with an idea. Since they had to reach their home, the fox being close by, one rat lay on his back and took the egg in his arms. Then, despite several lurches and false starts, the other pulled him by the tail.

Some animals, it seems, have more brains than many humans.

LA FONTAINE: FABLE

THE PRAIRIE OYSTER

Two cowboys were lost in the prairie without food or water. Eventually one of them succumbed to delirium through exhaustion and hunger, and to the alarm of his companion declared that he craved more than anything in the world to eat oysters. It seemed that there was no hope for the poor man, but as it happened fortune smiled upon him and caused his companion to stumble on an abandoned bird's nest full of eggs. These he gave to his demented friend who, mistaking them for real oysters, swallowed them and fell into a contented sleep. When he awoke he had miraculously recovered his health and his wits and the two were able to proceed with, and successfully conclude, their journey.

Today the Prairie Oyster is usually a somewhat more sophisticated pick-me-up. To make one, place in a small glass an egg, a teaspoon of Worcestershire sauce, a couple of dashes each of vinegar and Tabasco sauce, salt and pepper, taking great care not to break the egg. Then drink it, without stirring. This is supposed to be a foolproof cure for any 'morning-after' hangover.

It has also been suggested that certain eggs can act not merely as a pick-me-up but as an effective deterrent against drinking:

> The egges of an owle broken and put into the cup of a drunkard or one desirous to follow drinking, will so work with him that he will suddenly loathe his good liquor and be displeased with drinking.

SWAN: SPECULUM MUNDI, 1635

In China, thousand-year eggs are a highly prized delicacy. These are real eggs, preferably duck eggs, that are coated in a clay of ashes, lime and salt that preserves and colours them. Once coated, they are left for six to ten weeks while the chemicals from the surrounding clay soak into the shell. (The name 'thousand-year' is therefore a slight exaggeration.) At the end of this time, the egg's contents will have a

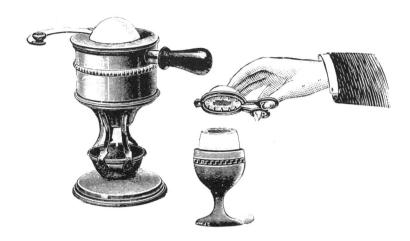

firm consistency and a smooth, creamy texture. Removed from its shell, a thousand-year egg should be translucent and brilliantly coloured in shades of blue and green; the yolk, in particular, will be a very vivid green. The coloration is in fact more reminiscent of onyx than of any type of food. The egg will have taken on a faintly fishy taste, and be very rich: half an egg per person is generally sufficient if there are other courses to follow. The Chinese usually serve these eggs cold at the beginning of a meal.

In the West, there is a renowned egg dish, traditionally served on Easter Day, called Scrambled Eggs Bentinck. To make it, take individual tartlet cases, as many as desired, and fill them with minced shrimps heated quickly in a little double cream. Pile on scrambled eggs and cover generously with cheese soufflé mixture. Bake in a hot oven until risen and brown and serve immediately.

EGGS FOR THE TSAR

Carl Fabergé, the son of a Swiss immigrant to Russia, was the favourite jeweller of every European court during the late nineteenth and early twentieth centuries. Above all, he was the jeweller whose work captured the imagination of Russia's ruling family, the Romanovs. Each year at Easter and other festivals, from 1884 to 1917, he would create exquisite jewelled eggs for the imperial family to present to each other.

These eggs were the product of a unique mind executed with marvellous skill. Made of precious materials, especially gold and precious stones, they had tiny secret springs which when released would reveal 'surprises' such as jewelled birds, models of imperial palaces, miniatures of the Tsar and his family, a tiny replica of the royal coach, a costly jewel, a locket or a tiny basket of spring flowers. Many of the eggs had tiny clocks set into them, and one was actually designed in the form of a rotary clock incorporating a star-scattered globe. It seemed that where eggs were concerned, the ingenuity of Fabergé and his master craftsmen knew no bounds.

The Orange-tree Egg shown here was presented to the Dowager Empress Marie Feodorovna by Nicholas II and dates from 1911. It is mounted upon a solid block of nephrite on which stand four nephrite pillars connected by gold chains. The 'soil' in the white quartz tub set with rubies and pearls is of hammered gold. The egg-shaped foliage surmounting the gold tree-trunk is made up of single carved nephrite leaves each engraved to show the veining. The flowers are of white opaque enamel with brilliant diamond centres. Among them are set precious stones including topaz, amethysts, rubies and diamonds representing fruit. When a small button is pressed the top leaves spring up and a gold bird rises from the inside of the orange-tree, sings, then disappears. The key to the mechanism can only be found by locating the right gem (disguised as a fruit) in the top of the tree.

MEDICAL EGGS

In Germany eggs were so scarce in 1918 that a doctor's prescription was needed to buy them. No doubt invalids then consumed them nicely soft-boiled; earlier they had been used for more bizarre remedies:

To break a Bile. Take the yolk of a newly-laid egg, some honey and wheat flour; mix them well together, spread it on a rag, and lay it on cold.

To draw a Rheum from the Eyes. Roast an egg hard: then cut out the yolk, and take a spoonful of cummin-seed, and a handful of bear's foot; bruise them, and put them into the white of the egg; lay it on the nape of the neck, bind it on with a cloth, and let it lie twenty-four hours, and then renew it: it will cure in a little time.

A Plaister for the Cholic. Spread the whites of four or five eggs well beaten on some leather, and over that strew on a spoonful of pepper, and as much ginger finely beaten and sifted; then put this plaister on the navel; it often gives speedy ease.

THE COMPLEAT HOUSEWIFE (LONDON, 1752)

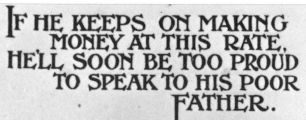

EGG PROVERBS

Eggs in the pan give pancakes but nevermore chicks.

The egg pretends to be cleverer that the hen.

Never a chicken comes from broken eggs.

Eggs not yet laid are uncertain chickens.

Old eggs, old lovers and an old horse,
Are either rotten or for the worse.

Tread carefully among eggs.

He who wants eggs must endure the clucking of the hen.

He thinks his eggs are of more account
than other people's hens.

One rotten egg spoils the pudding.

He who has many eggs scatters many shells.

Half an egg is worth more than all the shell.

THE COSMIC EGG

In the beginning neither Heaven nor Earth existed, only an egg-shaped chaos. From this egg a giant was born, called P'an-Ku. The heavy, dark yolk of the egg, the Yin, fell and became the Earth; the light, white part, the Yang, became the Sky. For 18000 years the Giant became bigger and bigger, and each day he pushed the earth and the sky further and further apart.

At last this great Giant died. His eyes became the Sun and the Moon, his voice the roll of Thunder; his breath the Wind and the Storm; his bones the mountain Rocks; his flesh the fruitful fields and the soil. Some ancient authorities say that the little fleas which hopped about his body were transformed into human beings.

Others say that the Giant was helped in his task of creating the world out of Chaos by a dragon, a tortoise, and a phoenix and a unicorn; and that before he died he made out of the elements little man-like figures and laid them out in the sun to harden. The first batch stayed out too long and burned black, so he put them to live in hot countries. The second lot were only half-baked, so these he sent to live in cold countries. But the last turned out just right, a delicious, golden yellow-brown; and these P'an-Ku placed in the fertile plains of the Middle Kingdom of China.

TRADITIONAL CHINESE FABLE

RUSSIAN EGGS

For many hundreds of years Russians have given eggs as Easter gifts; indeed, a nineteenth-century traveller to Russia remarked that 'scarcely any material to be named is not made into Easter eggs'.

Wealthy Russians would exchange beautiful jewelled eggs, crystal eggs and porcelain-painted eggs. Aristocratic Russian ladies would keep their hands cool by holding marble or jade eggs. Even those who were not rich exchanged Easter eggs, and during the days before Easter the streets would be filled with people giving each other these gifts. A delightful Russian folk tale tells of a young man who, carrying out his dying father's wish, distributes many Easter eggs to the poor on his way to church on Easter Sunday. At the church door he sees a poor old man and willingly gives his last egg. Then he realizes that the old man is Christ himself.

Children were often given decorated wooden eggs. Painted with scenes of children at play, they were a more practical gift for a child than a fragile egg shell. Children also enjoyed receiving 'nest eggs', which would unscrew to reveal another, smaller egg inside, right down to the tiny innermost egg: the principle is exactly the same as for the famous *matrioska* dolls.

Decorated wooden eggs were also popular with adults, and in the Ukraine these often had a brightly coloured geometric pattern painted on with a goose feather.

MAGIC EGGS

Eggs make wonderful 'props' for amateur magicians, as the famous French engraver Poyet knew. Did you realize that eggs can be made to obey – and disobey – their owners?

Take two raw eggs, drill a small pin hole in the ends of each shell and carefully blow out their insides. Leave the shells to dry, then pour some fine sand into one of them until it is about a quarter full. Conceal the holes with white wax and you have an egg that will balance no matter which way up you stand it. The sand inside will settle evenly on the bottom and keep it from rolling. This 'obedient' egg will do whatever you tell it.

To make your 'disobedient' egg, fill the other eggshell one quarter full with a mixture of sand and flakes of sealing wax. Seal the holes as before and heat the egg so that the wax inside melts and forms a solid with the sand in the narrow end of the egg. This egg will then only balance on its narrow end. No matter what other instructions you give it, it will stand only this way up. This is your 'disobedient' egg.

Another ingenious trick is the 'eggmobile'. What you most need for this is patience! Make a small hole in each egg and suck out the insides. Attach fuse wire to the eggs as shown. Heat the eggs gently and place them in cold water: they will suck in water as they cool. Attach metal thimbles to the eggs, stick a fork on each side of a cork and attach the eggs with more wire. Ensure the eggs' holes face in opposite directions. Place a coin on the bottle's mouth, stick a pin underneath the cork and balance the pin-head carefully on the coin. Pour a little paraffin into each thimble. If the eggs do not balance add little pieces of metal to the thimbles until the eggs are level. Light the paraffin and watch as the water turns to steam and the eggs are propelled in opposite directions.

POYET: LA SCIENCE AMUSANTE

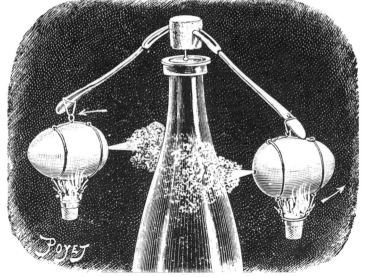

THE CUCKOO'S EGG

The hedge Sparrow's song is low and trifling it builds its nest
early in the Spring in hedges & close bushes green about
gardens of moss lined with fine wool & cowhair it lays five eggs
of a very fine blue ny it may calld a green blue they are clear
without spots it feeds on insects & small seeds & is frequently
robbd of its eggs by the cuckoo who leaves one of its own in its
stead which the hedgesparrow hatches & brings up with an
unconscious fondness & if she lays more eggs of her own after
the cuckoo has deposited hers it is said that the young cuckoo
has the instinct to thrust the young sparrows out of the nest to
occupy it himself wether this be true or not I cannot say for I
never witnessed it.

JOHN CLARE: NATURE NOTEBOOK

When coltsfoot withers and begins to wear
Long silver locks instead of hair,
And fat red catkins from black poplars fall
And on the ground like caterpillars crawl,
And bracken lifts up slender arms and wrists
And stretches them, unfolding sleepy fists,
The cuckoos in a few well-chosen words
Tell they give Easter eggs to the small birds.

ANDREW YOUNG

THE PHILOSOPHER'S EGG

The philosopher's egg is the crucible in which alchemists hoped to produce the philosopher's stone, a substance which would turn all other metals into gold or silver.

It is no accident that it was shaped like an egg, for the egg symbolizes the four elements: the shell is the earth, the membrane the air, the white the water, and the yolk fire.

In our picture the alchemist is not bothering with the refinement of a crucible, but attempting to create the philosopher's stone directly from the symbolic egg by destroying it with fire and a sword.

> Mine was the strangest birth under the sun;
> I left the womb, yet life had not begun;
> Entered the world, and yet was seen by none.
>
> OLD RIDDLE

EGG-BORN DEMONS

Among the less benevolent creatures that have hatched from eggs are the tengus. These goblin-like creatures lived deep in the forests of Japan. Though some tengus were shaped like men, others had bird-heads and were hatched from eggs. The chief tengu wilfully broke the Buddha's laws, but was forgiven after he had performed a penance.

Tengus were tiresome and malicious, no more than that, but other egg-born monsters were really evil. The basilisk, sometimes called a cockatrice or basilicoc, is a strange and dangerous mythical beast. In classical mythology, it is a serpent; elsewhere it is half serpent, half cock. Hatched by a toad from the egg of a cock seven years old, it can kill anything that moves simply by breathing on it or giving it the evil eye. It is said to be the offspring of the Devil and highly prized by sorcerers: the only thing that can destroy it is the cock himself, by crowing.

Inside an old cock is a white lump which looks like a small egg, so it is not surprising that cocks were supposed to lay bad eggs. In fact, the word 'cockney' is from the Middle English for 'cock's egg' – country people thought townsfolk were so badly nourished that they must live on cock's eggs.

Basilisks are much feared for the evil powers, but on a couple of occasions at least they have been brought to justice. In 1474 in Basle a cock who laid an egg was tried and convicted of sorcery: the unfortunate bird was burnt to death at the stake with its egg by its side. In 1538 a cockatrice was hatched in the cellars of Wherwell Priory in Hampshire and managed to devour several local people before being destroyed. The villagers did not forget it, however: a weathercock made in its image was stuck on their church as a warning.

EGG-BORN IMMORTALS

Many famous heroes, gods and goddesses have been born from eggs. Not least of these is Venus, who has mistakenly been portrayed emerging from a sea shell. One of the most remarkable births was that of the twins Castor and Pollux, who hatched out of the giant eggs laid by their mother Leda. The twins' father was Zeus, king of the gods, but as Leda was a married woman he appeared in her bedroom disguised as a swan in case the neighbours should start talking: hence, presumably, the eggs, which no doubt caused more of a stir than any number of lovers would have done.

> There was Chaos at first, and Darkness, and Night,
> And Tartarus vasty and dismal;
> But the Earth was not there, nor the Sky, nor the Air,
> Till at length in the bosom abysmal
> Of Darkness an egg, from the whirlwind conceived,
> Was laid by the sable plumed Night.
> And out of that egg, as the seasons revolved,
> Sprang Love, the entrancing, the bright,
> Love brilliant and bold, with his pinions of gold,
> Like a whirlwind, refulgent and sparkling.
>
> ARISTOPHANES: 'THE BIRTH OF EROS' FROM 'THE BIRDS'

The egg, the egg is round,
And the belly is round;
Come child in good health!
God, God calls thee!

ACKNOWLEDGEMENTS

The author and publishers are grateful for permission to quote the copyright extract from *The Kalevala*, reprinted by permission of the publishers from *The Kalevala, or Poems of the Kaleva District*, compiled by Elias Lönnrot, translated by Francis Peabody Magoun, Jr. (Harvard University Press, 1963).

The author and publishers are especially indebted to Venetia Newall for information obtained from *An Egg at Easter* (Routledge & Kegan Paul, 1971) in compiling entries on appliqué eggs, Easter messages and Russian eggs.

The author and publishers are indebted to the following for information in compiling entries entitled: 'The Cosmic Egg', fable from *Chinese Childhood* (produced by Blaketon Hall Ltd for Pollocks Toy Theatres Ltd and Barons, New York, 1977); 'Humpty Dumpty', from the *Oxford Dictionary of Nursery Rhymes* (Oxford University Press, 1951); 'Record Eggs', from Guinness Superlatives Ltd; 'The Philosopher's Egg', riddle quoted from *Voices* edited by Richard Wilbur (Penguin, 1970); 'Egg-born Demons' from the Victoria and Albert Museum.

Illustrations
The author and publishers wish to thank the following for permission to reproduce illustrations and photographs: Cooper-Bridgeman Library, page 47 (*Primroses and Birds Nests* by William Henry Hunt); Russell Coulson, page 13; Courtauld Institute of Art, page 53; Mary Evans, pages 7, 8, 9, 11, 21, 27, 32, 33 and 37; Forbes Magazine Collection, New York, page 35 (Orange-tree Egg by Fabergé); Linda Garland, page 15; Roger Garland, page 51; Ken Laidlaw, page 25; Barry Lewis, page 41; Mansell Collection, pages 6 and 17; James Marsh, pages 38–39; Venetia Newall, pages 19, 23, 43 and jacket; Terry Pastor, page 31; Mark Reddy, page 5; Scala, page 3 (*Danza delle Uova* by Mostaert); Victoria and Albert Museum, Crown Copyright, page 57; Christine Vincent, pages 54–55.

Designed and produced for G.P.Putnam's Sons by
Bellew & Higton Publishers Ltd
19–21 Conway Street London W1P 6JD

Library of Congress Catalog Number 80-81461
ISBN 0 399 12543 4
First American Edition 1980
Printed and bound in Spain

by Printer Industria Gráfica S.A.
Provenza, 388/Barcelona, San Vicente dels Horts 1980
Depósito Legal B. 16012 – 1980